A GATHERING OF KESTRELS

By

T.D. Keane

BLUE
CEDAR
PRESS

Blue Cedar Press
Wichita, Kansas

A Gathering of Kestrels   poems by T.D. Keane

Blue Cedar Press
PO Box 48715
Wichita, KS USA 67201

Visit the Blue Cedar Press website:
www.bluecedarpress.com
10 9 8 7 6 5 4 3 2 1

First edition April 2025
ISBN: 9781958728352 (paperback)
Library of Congress Control Number (LCCN): 2025931690

Editor: Michael Poage
Layout/Design: Gina Laiso, Integrita Productions

Printed in the United States of America

CONTENTS

Introduction

The poems in this collection were penned (yes they were actually penned) for the most part between 1987 and 1999. I know that's a long time ago, but I've been busy (at least that's what I've told myself to deny the fear of putting my poems out there for the world to see). In 1987 my wife and five-year old daughter and I had just moved to our new home, a 65-year-old frame farmhouse on ten acres in Wabaunsee County, Kansas. Our new home was fifteen miles (half gravel, half paved) from Kansas State University where I began teaching in 1984. As I was on a nine-month contract to teach in the Landscape Architecture Department, my summers were free to watch my daughter and become my old neighbor's dayworker and hay hand. George Crenshaw was around 65 when we first met and once he discovered that I had been putting up small square bales since the age of eleven or twelve we worked out a plan for me to help him with his hay. George would fertilize, swath, rake and bale my newly acquired seven-acre smooth brome meadow, an arrangement that would typically mean that two-thirds of the hay would be his and a third mine. The twist was that I took all the hay to sell to friends with horses and then worked for George to work off the two-thirds. We never traded a dollar and if it came out to where he owed me for the work, he would pay me in beef from one his registered black angus steers. On days where I wasn't helping load hay, I spent time in an open tractor seat atop an old wool blanket folded for backside padding and pulling a rotary mower, a disc, a chisel plow, and occasionally a 3-bottom moldboard plow. I also spent better than a fair amount of summertime with my young daughter and when she would watch a movie or be reading a book, I would take time to write.

In my teaching, my hunting and gathering activities, and time spent standing on a hay rack to stack bales I came to understand a fair amount about the Flint Hills, the landscape that we now inhabit. I have always defined my discipline (landscape architecture) as "the creative application of scientific understanding in order to craft a more sustainable inhabitance of place". The Flint Hills of Kansas are a magical place containing two-thirds of the remaining tallgrass prairie ecosystems left on earth with those ecosystems being arguably the most endangered on the planet. So, while I began to see this place through scientific and historical literature, I also sought to explore it through poetry.

By the late 90s I had some 60 poems composed and put them together in a "manilla folder" manuscript and shared this manuscript with a very few friends and asked for some feedback. Having no formal training or even a class in poetry I didn't know a pentameter from an anaphora (and probably still don't) and had no idea if what I had written had value or resonated with anyone else. Two friends I shared my work with are Richard and Vicky Hansen of Penrose, Colorado. I met them when Richard taught with us at Kansas State while Vicky completed her MFA in Ceramics. Once Vicky completed her graduate studies, she and Richard returned to their 40-acres with an adobe building complex in Southeast Colorado where they both began sharing a full-time teaching position at what was then called the University of Southern Colorado but is now known as Colorado State, Pueblo. At this writing, Vicky still teaches there, and Richard has retired. In our summer visits to the Hansen's place for flyfishing and sightseeing they informed me that one of the librarians at their university was the well-known poet, Tony Moffeit. Richard and Vicky said Tony was a kind of "beat" poet and performance artist. I assumed he was regionally known, it would be years later when I learned of his true stature as a poet.

I quote here from Todd Moore in his description of Tony Moffeit titled "American Blues Outlaw Poetry Anarchic Dream" to elaborate on Tony's place and force in poetry.

> "Tony Moffeit and I founded the Outlaw Poetry
> Movement in America in 2004, partly as a reaction
> to the kind of tame poetry generated by writing
> programs, academia, and the prize system which is
> good old boy, incestuous, and corrupt. However,
> Tony and I have been good friends since 1983
> when I published one of his early chapbooks
> entitled OUTLAW BLUES. But Outlaw in his work
> predates the early eighties because of his abiding
> interest in rockabilly, Delta Blues, Sun Records
> Country, and Hank Williams. Tony brought pop
> music culture to the poetry table when most everyone
> else was too cultured, too sophisticated to care."

I share this brief biography grabbed on-line as there is not much out there on Tony.

Tony Moffeit was director of the Pueblo Poetry Project in Pueblo, Colorado. He was the recipient of a National Endowment for the Arts creative writing fellowship in 1992. Also, in 1992, he was the recipient of a CoVisions grant from the Colorado Council on the Arts to give a performance program called "Poetry, Culture, and the Individual." In 1986, he was the recipient of the Jack Kerouac Award for his volume of poetry, Pueblo Blues, published by Cherry Valley Editions, Cherry Valley, New York. In 1997, he was the first-place recipient of the Denver Press Club's first annual Thomas Hornsby Ferril Poetry Prize. Both a literary and performance artist, Moffeit performed his original poetry and blues songs regularly with guitarist Rick Terlep.

In learning more about Tony Moffeit I kept thinking back to a poem by Robert Service titled "The Men That Don't Fit In".

Unbeknownst to me, Richard and Vicky Hansen shared my manuscript with Tony in early 2000, he read all the poems and was kind enough to provide a review which he typed and gave to the Hansen's. Richard then penned a letter to me and included Tony Moffeit's review with his letter. Tony's review was positive, supportive, and mentoring. He commented specifically on about two dozen poems which are included in this book, and he commented on my work in general, as well as the cohesiveness of the entire manuscript. I never got a chance to meet Tony Moffiet and to thank him face-to-face. Distance and my insecurities as a poet excused and precluded my contacting him and recent attempts to contact him have failed. My hope is that in some small way this collection of poems shows my gratitude for the inspiration he gave to me without my asking and for the courage he gave me to continue to write.

The poems in this work are about the land, the people who work with the land to sustain it and themselves, about working with your hands and simple (now antiquated to some) tools. They are about the others we share this unique place with and my journey (still ongoing) to come to know their stories. For I believe if we are to create a more sustainable inhabitance of place, we must know not only the names of the plants and animals, the rocks and the soils they yield, those who have come before and have followed; but we must also know their stories and hear their songs.

T.D. Keane

Canto

Walk softly on the prairie
        there are spirits resting there
The wind is their blanket
      the sage
            their prayer

Ruminations

If you wish to learn to write
        watch a cow
Slowly it grazes the field of ideas,
        then it swallows
The thoughts lie quiet, safely held,
        becoming richer, thicker
When time allows, they are brought back,
        chewed again
All nourishment is gleaned, and of course,
        there is some manure

Jan. 1

Again, I rose early
        dressed for the cold
        braced for the wind
I walked out to await the dawn

No sound, save the Earth's breaths
        heavy through the Cedars,
        a dull rasp on my cheeks,
short, anxious gusts, as if to say

Am I ready?
        for another trip
        around the sun,
with too many on my back

A brief lull,
        then long sighing note,
        perhaps the thought that we
are but a temporary (occasionally entertaining) disorder

The sun never showed,
        only the hale
        of a distant crow,
and glimpse of a bobcat

Notus

Her force is pure
        strong yet clean
Her power and subtlety
        rarely seen
but in waves of grass
        or twitching bough
in a ruffled feather
        or a ragged cloud

Old as mountains
        whose face she helped form
Fresh as a fawn
        frail, wet and warm
songbirds are silenced
        hawks dare not take wing
coyotes sleep in russet bowls
        and wait for night to sing

Her land's coat is furrowed
        combed clean of chaff and sin
I draw from her breath wearily
        as even sunlight bends
Some she strikes gracefully
        others she strikes true
what I seek most and only
        is to let her pass through

Scratch from me chaff
        worry and doubt
Winnow the random
        clutter out
partly dissolve me
        so that you may pass through,
become as much a piece
        of this place as are you

Canis lupus nubilus

A prairie ridge
bathed in fog and cloud,
stillness makes the silence loud

within the veils
of grey mists and blue,
trace of movement, a partial view

two yellow eyes
pierce morning haze,
search distant plains in mournful gaze

two ears erect,
head low to the ground,
she awaits the thunderous, forgotten sound

her body gaunt,
as air fills grey ribbed chest,
she howls an eerie song of death

A Cottonwood whispers
in russet valley below,
the wind is awakening, it's her time to go

The buffalo wolf
drifts with clouds to the East
the question remains,
          did I dream her or her me?

Thunder

What face wears the prairie
        this day in early May
Is it one of tranquil peace
        or one of tempest rage
It, of course, is neither
        but of both there is a trace

Thunderheads gather to the North
        preparing to come in
On the ground burns our backfire
        creeping gently into the wind
Flame and lightning now reveal
        as the sun's last rays dim

The South breeze goes flat
        the Earth's breath inhaled
Prairie waits in stillness
        for the storm's ensuing gales
Sage and Bergamot scent the air
        as birdsong wanes then fails

Caurus shatters the silence
        thunder and skyflash gain
Ground fire is given new life
        for yet there comes no rain
Dried grass and forb to the East
        prepare the strengthening flame

The fire explodes in embers and flares
         escapes its wind-drawn bounds
Its flows divide and surge uphill
in torrid dance of flame and ground
The peak in sight, it spreads and slows
         acknowledges the thunderous sounds

Crest now ablaze
         tongues reach for the sky
Lightning branches for the Earth
         from blackened crease on high
Glorious instant as the fires unite
         in the prairie's sacred tie

The storm rumbles East
         the grass flame subsides
Their strength now exhausted
         the passion declines
But image of this union
         will ever burn in these eyes

Crosscut

Bark cracks and splays
as the teeth gain bite
Now the rakers begin their work
    Sapwood shavings
    long and smooth
    Emerge from the deepening kerf

The sawyer wonders
if his aim is true
If he'll do justice to tree and search
    Fifty strokes
    then time for breath
    He ponders the sawlog's birth

He's taken measure
of this noble tree
Its size, the wind, its lean
    He's looked inside,
    guessed its grain
    Attempted to see that unseen

If he's measured wrong
the saw will bind
His work will be low and mean
    Fifty strokes
    then time for breath
    The sawyer begins to dream

Whose hands
have pulled upon this saw
Are his the first, or last
      How many men
      have sharpened its teeth
      Then given it set and cast

How each cut
is a journey of sorts
From present into the past
      Fifty strokes
      then time for breath
      He pauses now for rest

Scattered visions
fill his mind
Pores and concentric rings
      Growth and death
      shelter, hearth
      A perch for a bird to sing

Purpose, meaning
ashes and dust
Frost and the promising Spring
      Fifty strokes
      then time for breath
      What will the future bring?

The core now passed
the saw moves ahead
On its way to the down-slope side
      The sawyer's measures
      have proven true
      Wind and weight open kerf wide

Pay heed now
to crack and sway
That portend the felling tide
      Fifty strokes
      then time for breath
      Suddenly the tree bolts and dies

Good work
yet lies before
Conversion from tree to flame
      The sawing of bucks
      splitting and cord stacks
      As wood goes from wild to tame

The spark, the embers
the household warmth
And finally, an ashen fate
      Fifty strokes
      then time for breath
      Sawyer and wood, will end the same

Prairie Light

A narrow swath of salmon and rose
 above hills of violet and blue
A southwest breeze pushes clouds aside,
 a shaft of gold pierces through

Tawny russet coats of summer doe and twin fawns,
 grasses wine-red as they dry
Amber and pewter from sunlight and storm
 fight for control of August sky

Yellow beams on tanned forearms
 caked with warm olive chaff of alfalfa hay
Cream and green of antelope horn
 soft grey dancing shadows of cottonwood at midday

The prairie light paints
 with broad strokes and soft hues
Washes and surfaces easily seen
 but texture and richness oft hidden from view

No use is made of pure black or white
 just intermediate tones and casts
In-between colors and in-between shades
 appropriate perhaps, for an in-between land

But interest and mystery lie not at scales' bounds
 rather towards center where colors blend
In the harsh bright dull light of the prairie sky,
 in the quiet land the light lovingly rends

Concolor

To my south there lies a wildness
        that I have never seen
And yet on windless nights in March
        I am with her in my dreams

Her movement swift yet silent
her eyes pierce evening pall
She crouches low on a limestone ledge
        in wait for the deer to call

I watch as eyes look through me
        half-closed 'tween wake and sleep
Within, the flashes of predator mind
        as she dreams the deer to be

No movement does her body make
        save the rhythmic tail
Like a whisper, ears cup to the North
        as she scans the incoming trail

Faint cadence now of hooves on stone
        as the deer moves South to fate
Yet no motion but to lift her nose,
        best to be still and wait

From out of the night the deer appears
        her eyes begin to glow
Muscle and sinew tense, prepare the leap
        that portend the fatal blow

In less than half a heartbeat
     the deer is dead and down
The cougar's instinct honored
     and all without a sound

The lion moves off into the black
     kill clenched within her teeth
The dance of evolution
     performed for none to see

To my South there lies a wildness
     that I may one day see
Till then on windless nights in March
     I am with her in my dream

Hay Work

The forecast calls for a southwest wind
       and temps near a hundred all day
Already the air seems to stick to my skin
       as we head to the field to load hay

A meadow of swaying native grass
       now swathed, raked and sun-dried
An ocean of sixty-pound bales awaits
       seventy rods deep and ninety wide

Hook the hay rack to the tractor
       and the loader to the rack
Put on hay chaps and leather gloves
       stretch a stiff, aging back

The loader picks up the bales as we pass
       I grab each one by the twine
Stack them quickly, build the corners square
       keep the edges true and aligned

A poorly stacked load might not cross the creek
       the trail there is steep, and it bends
Aside from the beauty of a well-loaded rack
       it will keep you from loading it again

As I unload the wagon and reload the truck
       that will haul these prairie bales home
I hear in the distance the steady "clink-chunk"
       of old George and the bailer, alone

A hundred and twenty bales to a load
       five or six loads to a day
In the field it seems we'll never be done
       but too soon we are through with the hay

Diana

The marsh hawk appeared at dawn today
      sign that Autumn has arrived
The season of the hunt is upon me
      somehow, I come more alive

Three blue-winged teal have come to me
      offered their flesh for mine
A union of spirits has occurred
      in a way and place ill-defined

An ancient rhythm pulsates
      the cadence of Diana's clan
Songs of gathering, dances of pursuit
      old as the tribes of man

After the Harrier, the doe appeared
      followed by twin summer fawns
Cautious approach toward me she made
      yet sensing I meant her no harm

Silent bonds exist between hunter and prey
      connection of blood and mind
Melodies that can only be felt
      stanzas that cannot be timed

As I stand to leave water's edge this morn
      with sustenance of sinew and soul
A prayer is offered for the gift of the teal
      and the hunt that makes me whole

Adrift

What blindness this
      like transparent night
that screens the land,
        sacred Earth from sight

What silence this
      no more do we speak
to the spirits of the rocks,
        the soil and the trees

What deafness this
      that we cannot hear
the words carried by wind,
        the thoughts of the deer

What senses lost
      that we no longer greet
the music of water,
        the tides of geese

What?

Do we not ignore
      the wounding of land,
are we not numb
        to the scourge of man

Do we not mourn
      the loss of our home,
connections to family,
        fellow creatures as one

Do we not drift
        on a sea beyond earth,
unfettered, detached,
        from that that gives birth

Do we not long
for sacred sound,
the kiss of the grasses,
        caress of the ground

Do we?

If only one sense
        from our past we regain,
let it be the wisdom
        to feel the land's pain

Hyphae

Two thirds of the prairie, they say, lies underground
       within the soil, unable to be seen
In too rare moments of quiet contemplation
       I wonder
             if the same is true of me

A seemingly simple surface conceals
       complex networks of webs and ties
A conscious effort to keep most reserved,
       visible to
             only certain eyes

The grasses, they say, grow roots first
       to weather the harsh prairie climes
Fibers reaching into rich mellow earth
       where water
             and nutrients wait to be mined

As I live within this land
       my roots grow deep and true
That which produces the most
       it seems
             is most often hidden from view

Beacons

They take form in an instant
     like spirits becoming firm
Their sudden beauty startles
     each time I glimpse white birds

Reaction seems always the same
     whenever these beacons I sight
To pause, gasp in awe, then
     revel, in the mystery of flight

There was the time just down the road
     when dead willow gained new life
As a perched flock of glowing egrets
     erupted as one, into a storm-tossed sky

Hypnotic waves of pelicans
     that morning above the lake
The sound of a thousand wings foiling air
     as they hung, suspended in space

The barking skeins of snow geese
     pull dreams North to tundra sun
Pure light on glistening backs of white
     as nesting and teaching are begun

Avian omens of sorts, these birds,
     my inner peace they portend
Stray doubts and worries drain away
     as I watch them join with the wind

When they are gone, and I stand empty
     of life's concurrent dins
I wait on grace and wonder,
     will they come yet once again

That which gives life to the Sky

Like flowing sheets of silver
       the water's day begun
Reflected clouds and waltzing leaves
gilded gold by September sun

Lifeblood of the landscape,
       stand within a vein
Feel its pulse and power,
       join its patient grace

Always drawn to rivers,
this day with rod and fly
Though I revel in the pull of trout
       fish are but one reason why

To watch sky slide and tumble
       'neath willow bough and over stone
The dancing lights of the riffles,
       a torrent's sound, alone

Humbling strength of current,
       a turbulent, shifting bed
Mysteries lurking in dark water,
       yesterday's hatch, drifting, dead

Refraction of translucent color,
       distortion of landed view
Clarity of another realm
       ever the same, yet ever new

Just as gravity pulls the water
       the river beckons me
To sense life force and source,
       to dream of reaching my sea

Away

Where do we look
for life's needs, desires
for food, for shelter
for passion's fires
Away I say, Away

Where do we long
for comfort and peace
for God in her heaven
for Satan beneath
Away I say, Away

Where do we search
for the sacred place
for mountains, for seas
for desert waste
Away I say, Away

Yet all of these
are at our feet
in our own sunrise
in a freshening breeze

In soil at hand
all we could want or need
in the spirit of here
if we could but see

To this notion
of some other place,
of richer life elsewhere,
of a higher grace
Away I say, Away

Marsh hymn

Look first to the water,
                then to the sky
          be humble as you stare into the father's face

Pray quietly to him
                for an honest heart
thank him for this day, this place

Blend with the willows
                or the ripe marsh reeds,
honor that which you seek,
          wait patiently for grace

Reflection

The North marsh
seems sullen, darker and more somber
that it should at this time of day,
this time of the Fall,
this time of life

Cloud sky
slate-blue and grizzled by a Northwest wind
and a sun with too little heat,
too little fire,
too much uncertainty

Once supple willows
now rigid, bare, alone, strain in the gale
to free their feet from the grey ice,
the gelid muds,
to regain something lost

Just before sunset
the clouds retreat, the wind subsides and
a warm calm settles gently on the edges,
the folds,
the surface of the marsh

But within
the chilled heart longs, though it knows not why,
nor for what, for the death of winter,
the birth of spring,
or simply for joy

Cimarron

Jawbone of a beaver
in a shallow bowl of sand
front tooth split and yellow orange,
same color as the sunrise we watched this morn

Sweet spicy scent
of dried cottonwood leaves underfoot,
shortgrass, salt cedar, sage and sky
stones from another place, rounded, polished in history's water

Pain and joy
of yucca and hawk, cholla and quail,
magpies, prickly pear, jackrabbit and wind,
there is movement and life here, yet it seems ill at ease

Oil wells
gas wells, windmills, overgrazed range,
horizons converge as the whole place seems a mine,
pronghorns with colored collars graze alfalfa under a center-
pivot

This land's past
while much was wasted
was gathered and funneled into the pockets of a few,
thieves of heritage and hope dine boldly in the local cafes

A land in-between
a stolen past and an uncertain future,
a land that cycles between neglect and abuse,
always under the pall of exploitation, in dryness it waits

Devil's claw
in milo stubble planted in the dust
clash of human desires and land capabilities, I am uneasy,
The spirits are strong here, and though they grieve, they shed no
tears

Jawbone of a beaver
in a shallow bowl of sand
a hard, dry marker of a dry, hard land
but also, a memory of a soft, moist time, a time before greed

Dark Land

Grass, hill, and sky merge
as darkness blankets the prairie,
but as the blackness deepens an inner light grows

As vision drains away,
sound, scent, and touch flow in
to fill the void, to feel the night land

The coyote's song encircles,
thick and complete, rapt in
a musical shroud full of warmth and mystery

The night breezes,
hardly noted at mid-day
now caress with the grace of a familiar lover

Damp earth and grass,
yield rich fragrance of life and death,
cool air drains from the hills and flows to me

It is the hour of dreams,
they take form, assume life in the dark land,
the sun will return and be welcome, but come not too soon

Ash

Ashley's eyes looked up to mine,
I glimpsed the sparks of wisdom
so different from that which I might achieve,
so intimate with the Earth, the grass, the wind,
the birds

Her world so different,
sensed in shades of grey,
thousands of different sounds and scents,
a world in which she's earned intelligence, sympathy,
not so yet, of me in mine

She is as always, my teacher,
just as she is my friend,
Her devotion not only to my heart
but to my eyes, my ears, my soul,
and all that surrounds us

Each time that we hunt
and I follow in her wake,
I have less faith in the belief that human intellect
is somehow superior, the pinnacle, the gift of evolution,
rather it is but one, of the all

The Wall

The wall is built by mason and stone
  but not through force or will,
  rather it is the peaceful heart,
  patient ears and a humble skill

The stones have lain for ages
  perhaps waiting for the sun,
  now they lounge in scattered piles
  awaiting new life in the wall begun

The music of the stone's world
  where a measure may be years,
  notes are long, low and rich in tone,
  are they heard by modern ears

The stones will speak their strength and grain
  if one takes the time to hear,
  reveal their core to the inner eye,
  with images dark, but clear

The pace of the wall must approach the stone's,
  in patience we glimpse the soul, create art,
  begin to hear Earth's rhythms and chords,
  allow the stones to describe our part

This Place

What I care about
is this place, past times, past peoples
      this place, this time, these people
      this place, future times, future peoples, lives in
      this place

Before we can envision a "new tomorrow"
we must first address our past failures,
and our current transgressions, towards
      this place

Before we can live within healthy land
we must see and understand how
we have contributed to the land's illness, sickness of
      this place

We are not the land's disease, we are but the carrier,
and just as with human disease
      the carrier can be re-fashioned to cure
      that which it has caused, to ease the pain of
      this place

Grass

As the grass lengthens
      my height is lessened
As the sun brightens
      my darkness grows

As the wind freshens
      my strength decreases
As the current increases
      my movement slows

The willingness to become humble
      in the face of natures' forces
seems the first requisite
      of humanity

Terra

Last night I climbed the cuesta,
     as escarpment was gained
     I stood balanced,
between push of night wind
and pull of moon, facing full

Standing tall, swaying upon the cusp, I drank
     scent of the wild plum,
     song of the coyote,
decisions pondered then made, I jumped
and dove head-first into praryerth

My dream body swam in viscous soil,
     caressed by filaments and hyphae,
     drawing earth breath,
gently touching limestone bedrock,
amazed by images dark but clear

I settled on a shale ledge, soft stone,
     next to roots of a Cottonwood,
     waiting, listening, feeling
life flow of the rock and soil,
faint laughter of trickling ground water

Earth knows, this knowledge revealed
     as I lay rapt in its warmth,
     the soil cares,
I lay not in an inert body
but in a nurturing, compassionate world

Perhaps I will linger in this dark universe
     a placid realm of work and quiet,
     answers are never final,
only questions, yet I will return
for rest, new life without reservation

Necessary is Mystery

The field lies still and silent
  to feeble human ears,
  yet it beckons, welcomes, calls,
  brings the creatures here

Is it sound beyond our means,
  is it scent or slope,
  the way it blends the wind and light
  or some sense I'll never know

Three Sandhill Cranes, one early eve
  waltzed as they fed on grain,
  filtered sun on stone grey, blood red,
  beauty equals pain

A gliding flock of pinnated grouse
  descend from a November sky,
  truest of all the prairie birds
  remembering perhaps, another time

Cooper's hawks in aerial courtship
  dazzling flight and song
  pull my attention from cutting wood,
  make the winter seem less long

Turkey, pheasant, quail and owl,
  coyote, bobcat, hawk and deer
  the winged and four-legged visit this place,
  what force draws them here

A beacon masked to senses dull
  yet felt in soul and heart,
  glorious mystery of the natural world
  of which we are merely a part

Green Heads

Suddenly they cross the sky
        moving quickly South,
half-way across my dome of vision
before my eyes are caught,
        just as suddenly, time stops

A crisp afternoon, early fall,
        the air clean and the light
sharp as a freshly honed blade,
foliage resplendent, yet they trap
        my sight and I see only them

Their flight grabs, pulls,
        strains at my heart,
touches me in that place without name,
my body lightens and quickly
        I recognize the wind and wonder,

Ducks in high flight,
        details masked by distance,
provided by memory and dream,
green heads and violet-blue speculum,
        vivid as if in my hands

The South range of hills crossed
        and they are gone
so easy, effortless for them,
so difficult, painful for me,
        I mourn their passing

They leave me with envy
        for their freedom, their journey,
their singleness of purpose, resolve,
I long fully to be with them,
        yet just as fully to be here

Do they also envy
        my rootedness, territory,
my urge to stay, to see, to know,
as I lament and revel in our difference,
        I will watch the South range for their return

Temporal Voyage

Standing, firmly anchored
       on a shoreline ill-defined,
       waves awash in sunlight
roll in from the South beyond

Swells of amber and green
       consume the dark tones below,
       wind blending colors, textures
on a palette that flows and runs

Below are the remnants
       of the last ocean,
       one of water and warmth,
the sea I now watch is made of grass

This sea beckons me,
       upon it float my dreams, my prayers,
       whose tides I feel in my bones,
whose strength I know in my heart

An interim ocean,
       to be born anew as water or ice
       or nothingness, I wait
with the grass to become memory, dust, fossil

Cold Front

A tentative dawn
      of muted hues,
       a cold front on its way,
the land parched by summer sere
seems poised, anxious
        for the cool breath of the North

By mid-day
      the cool air
       preceding the front has arrived,
the humans fret and flit as if
the end of something is near
       and they are not prepared

At sunset
      clean and sharp,
       the front hits,
darkness and cold air reclaim the land,
reviving it, giving it rest,
       we do not own the land at night

In the cold dark
      the wind sings
       in fresh strong voice,
dreams emerge from the prairie soil
while grasses sway in their sleep,
       an owl calls and watches

Shadows

I fear not death
    for it has no power,
though its shadow lurks on the periphery
and its viscous body waits
    over the next range of hills,
I do not tremble

What I fear is
    lifelessness, loss of purpose,
the waning of strength, the ability to do good work,
the anticipation of sunrise and set,
    the promise of craft,
these bring night sweat

Yield not to fear,
    stubbornness is a virtue
in the face of uncertainty, in the dimness of the unknown,
utility is the blessing, futility the curse
    lean into the wind
and move on

For Henry

Let my eyes
　　　　see beyond surface or form,
　　glimpse the spirit,
　　the tendrils of life,
　　　　dreams withering and being born

Let my mind
　　　　distinguish the clever from the wise,
　　seek intelligence
　　with sympathy,
　　　　as you directed: "simplify"

Let me be
　　　　composed of discipline and grace,
　　a heart of tender chastity,
　　an unspoken poet
　　　　with a warrior's face

Pain

I seek no solace in your arms
        nor in your eyes
Grant me merely understanding,
        silent empathy,
        a crooked smile

Memory remains when all else fails,
        as it should
The strength of thought and love
        is all that matters
        in the world of men

Cottonwood

Sometimes they stack up
       fears, concerns, misconceptions, angers
Like cordwood, hastily piled,
       shoddily stored, gravity ignored
And one worries if they will collapse
       or rather, when

As always there is a decision,
       let them fall, perhaps injuring those near
Or knock them down,
       discard the inferior and carefully place
Those that matter, those that will rest
       in silence

Today's choice was informed
       by a young cottonwood, a ventured life
Growing in a fence line
       four, five, perhaps seven years old,
In a precarious position
       yet unashamed, untimid

An expression of joy,
       branches spread, leaves dancing
Sunlight glinting, scattering in the wind,
       a tree in danger, yet laughing
Singing to the day,
       scenting the air with spice

I will learn from this tree,
       each day is precious
Disregard the darkness,
       dance in the light and laugh,
Stack well that which matters,
       ignore the fall

Windsong

A strong Northwest wind
        late March
      last Fall's leaves and chaff dancing

A rusting windmill
         no longer functional
      sighs with each piercing gust

Try as I might
        to ignore analogy
      I hear the cries of a dying women

Strange how a machine
        product of steel and physics
      can give voice to the land

Partners

Life and death are wed,
      inextricably linked, partners on the journey,
to fear one is to fear both,
      yet we see one as a gift
      the other as a taking away,
Are we not half blind

For if no one mourned our passing,
      if no one regretted our death,
if we had no remorse
for those left behind,
would not death
Be the most joyous of all gifts

Strata

A landscape of layers,
        some seen and some only sensed
There are the rock, the soil, the grass
        the four-legged, the winged, the sky

But there are also the memories,
        the remembrances of this land,
Such history lies thick on the flats
        and is carved deep in the draws

Fissures of memory
        inscribed by water and wind,
Details etched in the bank walls
        but dulled by years of drought

Roots and stone
        recall the passing of the bison,
The bugle of the bull elk,
        the soft steps of the grizzly

Cottonwood and coyote
        are the storytellers of this land's tribe,
One relays the wind's poems,
        the other sings of the prairie soil

The shamans of the clan
        are yarrow, bee balm, and sage,
Their medicine heals land wounds,
        their scents carry land prayers

Each member of the land tribe
speaks of its history, portends its future,
If we will but stop and listen
        perhaps we will be invited, to rejoin this clan

Looking

Often, I step outside,
      look back, within
Just as often
      the view disappoints
But what if it did not
      would I still step outside
      look back,
      within

Will the view ever please,
Is corrective work
      possible, worthwhile,
      warranted
Will standards
continually rise, fall
Who decides,
      why

Perhaps when stepping out
      my focus should be
      forward, without
Could I walk
      to the possible
Limp and stumble
      to what can be,
      forget what is

Rainshadow

Four days of gentle rain,
grey skies and somber outlooks,
      day and night
      lack clear demarcation,
the sun refuses
to slice the pall

A sea of general malaise,
broken by swells of depression,
      I miss the wind's strength,
      the sharp light,
the crackling of dry grass
beneath my steps

Are my spirits controlled
by air pressure and irradiance,
      do demons wait for gloom
      to plague my thoughts,
and why do I find
this prospect so comforting

Blue Eyes

When I am at peace
        and wish to truly see
I close my eyes
For the imagery of memories
        connected through darkness
is more vivid than momentary perception

Just as the red wine matures,
        its complexity and intensity
growing with time
So too of my visions,
        my remembrances,
my depth of clarity, of sight

I see the lustrous grey
        of flint shards,
glistening on the damp prairie soil

Switchgrass, yellow-orange,
        shot full of light and life
from a Southwest sun

Skeins of geese and ducks
        crossing an October sky
so blue it stings the eyes

Pallid skin of chilled fingers
        stained with the blood
of prairie birds

I see the cream and tan
of native limestone,
soft rock with its own memories

The gleaming white rump
          and ink-dipped primaries
of the Harrier in low flight

The limbs of a bur oak
          embracing a golden dawn,
straining with weight of dew on leaves

December clouds, laden with snow,
          barely able to clear the South range,
will they carry their burden past?

I see streams of flame
          flowing towards the draw
where the grass grows dense and tall,
The wind infuses the fire,
          creating a crescendo of colors, sounds and scents,
in its wake, only black

I see the face of a coyote
          as we interrupt each other's hunt,
amber eyes show surprise yet humor,
Her pewter and russet coat
          rippling as she lopes off
to consider our little joke

All this and more I see
          when I am at peace
and my eyes are closed
Perhaps what they say is true,
          that blue eyes
do see better in the dark

Too Still the Morning

At dawn I left to walk the land
seeking game with gun in hand
      Yet, last night's dream held in mind
      perhaps its root I sought to find
In mystery and clarity's grinding mill,
On such a morning much too still

Remorse, regrets always fall away
each time I view a freshening day
      Yet, a shadow trailed a half-step behind
      was it the dream's or was it mine
No one can say what shall or will,
On such a morning much too still

Pond and streams bereft of life
simply reflect a stagnant sky
      Heavy dew refuses to fall
      no zephyr stirs, no none at all
No woman's breath could stay the chill,
On such a morning much too still

Flat iron clouds of pewter and grey
in a North sky pressing night into day
      Eve passed or new morn, which shall I grieve
      air lies heavy as I struggle to breathe
Will I seek to learn or merely to kill,
On such a morning much too still

I bow barbed wire to cross the fence,
walk the draw where the grass grew dense
  Stop, catch a thought, extend the dream,
  suddenly the pheasant explodes from my feet
A hunter's instinct more than skill,
On such a morning much too still

A brazen bird in pallid air,
a blaze of color in a land austere
  The gun is shouldered, shot slices the pall
  intercepts arc of flight, causes the fall
A reverent exchange or simply a kill,
On such a morning much too still

Mystery and thanks blend in my chest,
I heft the pheasant from its place of rest
  As I stroke feathers a wind gently speaks,
  the land is alive for those who can see
I've seen so little of the all, all I never will
On such a morning of grace and life,
  a morning no longer still

Stalking

Come bathed in sunlight
       or through the stillness of dawn
Pass gently on a Southwest breeze,
         evade me in a low prairie draw

Mix with scents of wild plum in May
       or the voice of a Redtail in flight
Allow but a glimpse in the trickle of springs,
        stay outside the fence that is night

Spirit of these Flint Hills, bluestems, the Kaw,
       more simply spirit of this place
Eternal, ephemeral, humorous and spry,
        I sense your presence, but not yet your face

Old Flames

To sit patiently, quietly
and watch a fire rekindle
from coals to flame
is a lesson in passion
tenderness, love sustained

The embers, red showing
through grey, seem cool
tired, thoroughly familiar,
yet they retain a hidden wildness,
an uncertain certainty

New wood, dry and longing
is placed atop the coals
and stoked by the breath
of the firekeeper, the yield
at first, only smoke

But through the grace
of waiting the flame appears,
slow at first, preceded by
the scent of the oak,
and one wonders

Will the flame grow
or subside, will it
enrapt or extinguish
and then, as through
faith, it explodes

The wood is suddenly
caressed by flames,
a crescendo of fire
as it shifts position
obeying gravity's beck

And again, there is warmth
heat, gratitude and solace,
there is assurance that
things go on, that there
is always new, in the old

Mystery Meat

Reluctantly
I must admit my appetite for facts
I savor their crispness, clarity
I relish their intense, singular flavor
I store them away,
  their resurgence frequently surprises me
Like sugar, salt, pepper
  they are basic to the soup of discussion

Less reluctantly
I admit to the attraction of the unknown,
  the unknowable
I am drawn to the abyss
  at the edge of knowledge
My lack of discernment
  of the spices and stock of mystery
  only makes the stew all the richer

Wisdom, it seems
  is not derived from what one knows,
  but from knowing what you don't,
  and never will

Call it, in the air

As does the moon,
the soul has two sides
       That which is shaded, glimpsed,
         but open to the scrutiny of light
And that which is shielded
covered, kept hidden from all, even himself

I have found that the brighter shines
       the former,
the deeper the darkness of
       the latter

Got a minute?

We think the minutes precious
        yet the days slip idly by
Perhaps a symptom
        of a distorted sense of time

"Time is Money" we are told,
        what rot, what lunacy
Both are mere abstraction,
        neither currency

Vision?

Walking, thankfully walking
      over familiar ground
      through unfamiliar air
A September fog
      lies thick and heavy
      rendering morning sky to mere memory

As I move on
      a circle of vision
      thirty yards across travels with me
Navigation is by microtopography
      small dips and rises,
      a patch of white sage, ironweed, a hedge post

I seem to know each
      know just where I am
      yet have no memory of learning these cues
Perhaps my body
      has gathered these fine details
      while my mind and eyes have been elsewhere

I reach a corner
      of pasture and field
      crossing the wire gate, the scent of damp earth
Turning South at the pond
      walking, listening, breathing
      I skirt the creek and the sloughgrass

A pheasant breaks
        from cover of bluestem and gramma
        I see it with my ears, color it with memory
A raucous bird
        out of my range of sight
but full in view

I crest a stock pond dam
        come nose to beak, eye to eye
        with a great blue heron who springs at once
The heron makes not a sound
        as she heads East
        is she real or dreamt? I can see her

Just as the heron
        disappears into the viscous air
        a fait creak of wing joint proves substance
Two birds,
        one seen clearly with ears and memory,
        one seen dimly with eyes and question

Out of the fog comes clarity
        less seen
        more perceived
Trust in that
        we don't know we have, don't know we can do,
        thank the fog for its lesson and walk on

Poor Land

It's not a pretty piece of land,
        does not stand out among its peers
It's disheveled, unkempt, disarranged,
        abused and uncared for
Its skin is blemished with a thousand
        small cedars, its flesh
        cut to the bone by years of
        hard rain and hard use

Considered singly, it's poor land,
        yet as Aldo noted
Often poor land is rich country and
        part of what makes country rich is context
Neighbors, surrounds, inhabitants
        landscapes of compatriots, friends
        supporters, we are rich only in
        relation to these

It's a vulnerable piece of land,
        open to further abuse, damage, death
It's capable of paying long after its heart
        quits beating (like life insurance)
It's caught the eye of the quarry man
        who seeks to peel its skin
        strip the bones, crush them
        and scatter them for all to tread

It's owned land, private property,
  whose owner has legal right to kill
The rocks, the soil, the grass and trees,
  all to do with as they please
Who can own rocks, grass, the land,
  can we hold the spirit of a place
  in our hands or lock it away
  in a safe deposit box

This land will be killed with the pen,
  the quarry man will conduct the post-mortem
The land they say will be reclaimed,
  yet we know it will be but an empty shell
We will drive our cars and pick-ups on its bones
  with nary a thought of their source,
  what they once founded, supported,
  without tears for the loss of another neighbor

Redtail

I've seen your face
a thousand times,
   give or take a few
Though your raiments
are rarely the same,
   your eyes tell me it's you

I've seen your head
pale as driven snow,
   or dark as a moonless night
Your breast often mottled
brown, buff and grey,
   or glowing a pure shining white

A spreading tail
of fervid umber,
   as it turns to wind and sun
Wings broad, mighty
foil prairie air,
   as another hunt is begun

But always the eyes
searching the keep,
   windows to predator soul
Soft yet firm
vicious, detached,
   qualities I long to know

A secret yearning
to trade our roles,
   survival for responsibility
A mouse for a dollar
a snake for a deed,
   worries, for a death that is free

Fall Line

Drop gently
      to the bluestem blade,
      flatten, spread and slide
      to the joint of stem and leaf
Wait for others to join,
      then begin your voyage
      back to the sea

Run quickly
      to the soil, to shelter
      from sun and wind,
      in the voids, the hollows of earth
Gather mineral, acid, humus,
      then carry these gifts
      to the plants or the stream

Carve a new valley,
      polish an old stone,
      carry a caddisfly
      to the waiting trout
Merge with frozen brethren
      in a deep blue glacial flow,
      roll off glistening fur of an otter

A million mystic journeys
      all yours to choose,
      each with the same
      beginning and destination
Travel each and all
      so that we may be,
      but please, enjoy the ride

Artifacts

An ice-blue plastic bag,
      black lettering
      and a yellow disc with eyes and a smile
      catches a gust of wind
      and dances briefly above
      the hot August pavement
The smiling face likely
      gladdened the purchaser
      of whatever the bag once contained,
Whom does it gladden now?

A brown glass bottle,
      red and white label
      in a tattered paper sack
      lies partially hidden by
      the weathered grass and
      the blooming ragweed
The contents of the bottle
      perhaps quelled the past
      or staved the future,
Whom does it wait for now?

A frayed jag of rubber,
       steel and rayon cords
       lie baking in the sear
       materials from a tree and the earth,
       the remnants of raised letters
       suggest the word "year" or "stone"
Did the tire explode
       or slowly come apart
       with sound or sensation,
Where is the driver now?

All these discarded objects,
       we think and thus see
       as trash, refuse, scabs of unhealed wounds,
       yet we view the glistening black
       of the asphalt or the shimmering white
       of the concrete as necessary, good
A vulture sits atop
       the crossmember of a powerline pole
       and sees it all as damage, scar and possibility,
Whose perspective is valid?

Sky Keepers

A vortex of ring-billed gulls (Larus delawarensis)
    climbs and slides
    above a field of red milo
    ablaze in the October sun

A single Kestrel (Falco sparverius)
    nervously hovers
    above a roadside ditch
    waiting for movement to reveal prey

A thousand Snow and Blue Geese (Chen caerulescens)
    break ranks and fall
    from an ice-blue sky
    to a sodden February corn field

Whether one or many,
    in sight or in dream,
    wing beats purchase lift,
    blood, muscle, to grace, mystery, beauty

Their presence, movement
    give depth to firmament,
    their wings give heft
    and substance to the wind

Bless the keepers of the sky,
    may they always soar
    through the sharp-edged
    prairie light, and the darkness of my dreams

You are Here, Standing

Here it is that we stand,
      but upon what,
      for what,
      what is it that founds this standing?

In the times before,
      what we were
      was determined
      by where we were and where we had been.

In these times
      do we stand on rock,
      or shifting sand,
      on the green of money, or on that of new grass?

Do we note
      the seasons' change
      by bird and flower,
      or by calendar, clock, and catalog?

Are we formed
      by here and history,
      or do we form them,
      from ignorance and the arrogance it spawns?

Place makes culture,
      our downfall it seems
      will be,
      our unfounded belief in the inverse.

Exam II

How seldom I listen
        to the breath, the fears,
        the concerns of my students
How rarely I observe
        their victories, defeats
        while they occur

Usually I talk,
        surrounding myself
        with a barrier of speech
An opaque wall
        that obscures, distorts
        clarity, fidelity, perception

But today I hear,
        though they give voice
        to not a word
I see clearly,
        though they neither
        display nor present

Their heads are down
        pencils, pens moving quickly,
        attempting to relate
In their efforts to convert
        blank space to meaning, proof,
        they speak, they perform

While they vary
        in their grace, their tone
        they all dance, all sing
Perhaps the most profound
        sights, the richest songs
        come in silence

Draft

Kansa, "people of the South wind",
     It is their land I now inhabit,
though they are gone
the wind remains,
     perhaps it still carries their voice,
thoughts, fears, concerns, joys,
given form, breath,
     and shared with the prairie air

Tonight, as I lie awaiting sleep
     I listen to the South wind,
hear its song, sense its spirit,
its music is strong, forceful,
     it trumpets through cedar boughs,
loose window sashes provide the tympany,
power lines blend in the cello chords,
     the melody rich yet foreboding

Out here, the wind is noticeable
     more in its absence
It becomes a companion,
when it's not with me,
     not there to support my strides,
I tend to list a bit
The old-timers, whether trees or ranchers
     all stoop a little from leaning into it

We sing its praises in July
     as it quells the stagnant heat,
curse it in March
as the skin of our fingers split
     and our souls seem forever chilled
but tonight, I neither thank nor chastise,
for it carries a message,
     one heard by the former inhabitants

71

The words the wind brings this night
           are those of change, of warning
Its mother earth and father sun
are moving apart, becoming distant,
           the equinox passed and the solstice
is but two nights hence
It will sound no more this year,
           but retire, reflect, regain its strength

A long mild Autumn is over,
           The South wind heralds its death
and promises to yield
to its sister from the North
           whose palette contains little
but grey, black, and white,
whose music loses interest
           in its repetition and rhythm

Just before sleep overtakes me
           I express whispered gratitude
to the South wind for its spirit,
for its wisdom and humor,
           I beg it rest not too long,
come in Spring to fuel the prairie fire,
to color the grass, the sky, and make them dance,
           to thaw my heart, melt my soul, and allow me
                       one more laugh

Prevarication

I have grown weary of
        and will have no more hand
        in monuments to man,
whether they be fabricated of stone
        or of words

Let my purpose be
        monuments to the Kestrel,
        tributes to the bluestem,
commemorations to water, sky, soil,
        humor and death

        for these are such
        as will outlast
human edifice,
        and ego

Support

A common rafter,
two by six of pine or fir,
unpainted and set in place
by unskilled hands

A single member,
yet part of a team,
that supports a shed roof
sheathed in metal

Nails hastily placed
and shoddily driven,
the construction displays neither
craft nor compassion

Yet it is here
I find beauty, grace,
springing not from human ineptitude,
rather from what the rafter holds

Common materials
in uncommon construction,
mud and black horsehair,
bits of straw and feather

Woven together,
laid up in beaded rows,
half circles that increase in radius
from base to cusp

The swallows art,
founded by function, purpose,
as all art should be, perhaps,
yet arresting, soothing

The beads of dried earth
resemble those seen elsewhere,
on the brow tines and main beams
of the buck deer's antlers

What is it about
this "style", this native fabrication
that provides strength, rigidity,
fleeting permanence?

Shafts

The left side of my brain
seeks explanations,
the angle of irradiance,
the clarity of the atmosphere,
changes in reflectivity ratios

> while the right side
> revels in the mystery
> of Fall light,
> the movements it triggers,
> the subtleties it reveals

The cant of the sun's rays
in late September,
could they be the catalyst
as they strike my retinae,
remix the chemical cocktail

> these golden shafts
> are longer, cleaner,
> cause the migration of geese,
> the descent of elk,
> the drift of memory and dream

An evolutionary vestige
like the appendix,
once necessary, now atrophied

> the ability to see the light,
> to listen to its message?

Red Oak

Red Oak
Quercus rubra,
(formerly Quercus borealis maxima,
a name with greater majesty)
is uncommon in these parts,
in these grasslands,
in these Flint Hills,
around here

Even though
it is rare, unusual,
unique, it does not stand forward,
announce its rarity or status,
it reveals itself only
to close observation
of riparian corridors
of woodland

Except
for now, this time,
this part of the Fall,
this precious end of October,
warm days, cool nights,
sunlight so pure, crisp
that it can penetrate
the soul

Changes
have begun,
nutrients withdrawn, sent below,
chemical conversions resulting
in bronze, copper, ferrous red
foliage that laps irradiance
and fractures its colors
for my eyes

Grace
honest differentiation,
its show of brilliance is not
calculated, timed for maximum impression,
rather it is the result of work,
the tree's calling, vocation
preparation for dark rest
and for rebirth

A Gathering of Kestrels

Two filaments of steel
      span the space
between glass spools
      affixed to dead conifers
stripped of bark and branch,
      replanted at the side
of a seldom traveled
      township road

The poles and road
      run due East, or West
straight as a taut line
      in the horizontal,
but in the vertical
      they climb and dip
with the heave and swell
      of these Flint Hills

The cuestas repeat
      into the distance
like a canyon echo
      that goes silent at the horizon,
but on a ridge, on the road,
      on the wires on a September morn
I happen upon
      a gathering of Kestrels

Little coyotes of the wind,
      and just for an instant
I can see their wake,
      their aerial trail,
clear as water parted
      by beaver, boat, or bug,
the pattern not one
      of purpose or predation

Rather it is one of
          exuberance, laughter, pure joy,
like an otter's tracks
          in the streamside snow,
Perhaps we have trouble
          seeing the grace in the
lives of kindred animals,
          perhaps we miss their elation

Because we have
          so much trouble
finding these
          in our own lives,
I wonder what
          they make of
our tracks, our trails,
          markings upon the land

Stray thoughts

Wisdom, it seems to me
is assembled, gained, engendered, fostered,
learned, or earned
       while listening

It might be shared when speaking,
       briefly

It might be gauged
by how much one says,
       or how little

            Lo what wonders one can see
            if they will but sit quietly,
                   to watch a new-born sun arise,
                   look with your heart,
                   hear with your eyes

quiet

I speak but one language
but am fluent in the silence of many

The beauty of quiet,
universal, meanings similar in all languages,
present or past.

Only in silence can one hear,
absorb, consider; perhaps understand

And only in listening
can one assemble the wisdom needed
to lead them through.

www.ingramcontent.com/pod-product-compliance
Lightning Source LLC
Chambersburg PA
CBHW071035050426
42335CB00050B/1705